OBERON BOOKS
LONDON

First published in 2000 by Oberon Books Ltd.
(incorporating Absolute Classics)
521 Caledonian Road, London N7 9RH
Tel: 020 7607 3637 / Fax: 020 7607 3629
e-mail: oberon.books@btinternet.com

Zozòs (Cuckoos) was first published by Gremese books in a collection of Manfridi's work entitled *Theatre of Excess*.

A catalogue record for this book is available from the British Library.

ISBN 1 84002 151 9

Front cover photograph: Tom McShane

Back cover photograph: Elio Carchidi

Series Design: Richard Doust

Printed in Great Britain by Antony Rowe Ltd, Reading.

Giuseppe Manfridi

Giuseppe Manfridi was born in Rome in 1956 where he now lives after several years in Paris. For the past fifteen years his work has been constantly produced on the Italian stage. His first major hit was *Giacomo il Prepotente* (Giacomo the Petulant) about the poet Giacomo Leopardi, which opened in 1989 at the Teatro Stabile di Genova and for the next three years played throughout Italy. This was followed by the equally successful *Ti amo, Maria!* (I Love You, Maria!) which was turned into a film. Other notable successes have been *La Partitella* (Kickabout) and *Teppisti!* (Hooligans!) which approach the Italian obsession with football in starkly contrasting ways. Manfridi returned to the subject of football violence with his monologue *Ultrà* which he later adapted into a screenplay of the same name; the film, which was directed by Ricky Tognazzi, won the Golden Bear for the best film at the Berlin Film Festival in 1990.

Other successful plays include *La Cena* (The Dinner), *Elettra* and *L.Cenci*, as well as *Zozòs* (Cuckoos). Manfridi's work has been produced in France, New York, Greece, Canada, South America and Finland (where the Manfridi Theatre in Helsinki is named after him). In 1998 *Giacomo il Prepotente* opened at the prestigious Theatre des Champs-Eliséés in Paris.

Preface

Manfridi and the Theatre of Excess

Theatre must always be credible, capable of winning and holding the belief of the audience; though from the Greeks on, this has never meant avoiding the shocking, the fantastic or the plainly horrible. To balance dangerously on the edge of rejection has always given an excitement to the theatre that helps it communicate. Convention must always be challenged, even if it is on the brink of the sensational. So Titus Andronicus cuts his hand off on stage; Gloucester has his eyes pressed into a vile jelly; Howard Brenton's Romans bugger the British and create a horrible image of colonial exploitation; Oedipus gouges out his eyes off stage, but displays the bloody sockets to the audience immediately afterwards. The classical theatre has always shocked us with excess. And generations of censors have always tried to prevent it.

The contemporary Italian dramatist Giuseppe Manfridi aims to reclaim this territory for modern drama. He is fond of extreme events. He lets the Theatre of Excess into an ordinary apartment and, by bringing its horror up-to-date, gives us a shock which makes an ancient myth startlingly modern. He makes something new in the theatre by appropriating the very old.

Manfridi's Theatre of Excess pushes our suspension of disbelief to the limit. There is a plain ordinariness about these amazing stories which makes the audience believe. It all seems so 'real'. Of course, the audience know that the events are not real, but they want their ability to imagine to be respected. What happens on stage must be credible, however disturbing it may be. In that sense it must be true in its artifice. One of the most tawdry phrases in the theatre is 'getting away with it' when applied to an inadequate piece of business, an unclear speech, or a creaky turn of the plot. Manfridi never gets away with it: he confronts it. And out of this is born excess.

The journey of *Cuckoos* is amazing. What other modern play starts as sexual farce and ends as horrific tragedy? Is it a throwback to the Theatre of the Absurd? No: it is very real. So is it <u>sur</u>real? No: it always remains real. The premise of *Cuckoos* is as disturbing as anything in modern drama; its conclusion takes us right back to the Greeks.

Peter Hall
London 2000

Characters

BEATRICE
a woman of about forty

TITO
a man of about twenty

TOBIA
a man of about forty

Note: this playscript went to press before opening night and therefore may differ slightly from the text as performed.

Cuckoos was first performed in English at The Gate Theatre, London on 21 March 2000, in association with The Royal National Theatre Studio's Springboards initiative, with the following cast:

BEATRICE, Kelly Hunter
TITO, Paul Ready
TOBIA, David Yelland

Director, Peter Hall
Designer, Lucy Hall
Lighting Designer, Neil Austin
Sound Designer, Steve Morgan

Casting Director, Sam Jones
Assistant Director, Rebecca Gatward
Assistant Designer, Loukia Minetou
Stage Manager, Julie Derevycka
Deputy Stage Manager, Emily Danby
Assistant Stage Manager, Atalandi Aperghis
Set Builder, Simon Plumridge
Photography, Pau Ros

GATE   For The Gate Theatre:

Artistic Director, Mick Gordon
Executive Director, Philippe Le Moine
Associate Director, Rebecca Gatward
Producer, Tara Hull
General Manager, Sarah Preece
Production Manager, Greg Piggot
Technical Manager, Jo Walker
Administrator, Christine Morin
Literary Manager, Katherine Mendelsohn

NT spring boards   For The Royal National Theatre Studio:

Head of Studio, Sue Higginson
Studio Manager, Matt Strevens
Technical Manager, Eddie Keogh
Assistant to Head of Studio, Nikki Young
Press Representative, Lucinda Morrison

ACT ONE

The stage is in semi-darkness. A shaft of light comes from the half-opened bedroom door, stage left. The living room of a small flat is partially visible. It is very untidy. The furniture and various items are strewn all over the floor. In the background there is a corner for cooking. Stage right, a hall door. From the bedroom there emerges the excited voices of a man and a woman that gradually and painfully grow nearer over the following exchange.

BEATRICE: Well, where's this parachute then?

TITO: What's wrong with the sheet?

BEATRICE: The sheet?!

TITO: Or my dressing gown –

BEATRICE: That's filthier than the sheet. Where's the parachute ?

TITO: You should relax, you know?

BEATRICE: Relax?! If you were in my position – ?

TITO: I am in your position.

BEATRICE: I have some standards still. And your bedlinen and casual attire fall considerably short of those standards.

They have stopped at the door. A shadow can be seen.

TITO: But it won't be for long.

BEATRICE: It won't be at all, do you understand? I simply refuse to parade myself –

TITO: It's just my old man.

BEATRICE: Just your old man!

TITO: But that's why we called him.

BEATRICE: All I need, some filthy old man –

TITO: My Dad's not filthy.

BEATRICE: Like father, like sheet. Ahh…

TITO begins to pant.

Not again!

TITO: I'm afraid so.

BEATRICE: Stop it, just stop it. It's you, you know, it's your fault, it's all coming from your end.

TITO: (*Trying to contain himself.*) It's not, it's yours, it's your end that keeps contracting.

They collapse through the bedroom door onto the stage. They are in an unequivocal position. However, their nudity and, above all, the crudity of the position is masked by the dim light and a piece of cloth which they hold over themselves.

Ahh…

BEATRICE: Well, let's hope that's the end of it! Now, since we've started, let's keep it up.

TITO: Isn't that the problem – ?

BEATRICE: The momentum. Keep the momentum up. May the Lord protect us from *double entendres*.

TITO: What about my gym towel?

BEATRICE: I want the parachute! I want the damned parachute! (*She stops.*) There is a parachute, isn't there? Don't tell me you don't have a parachute? You never did make any parachute jump, did you?

TITO: I did. I do. I wasn't lying. It's there. It's just that –

BEATRICE: What?

TITO: It's nothing… When Dad arrives, he could get it for us.

BEATRICE: No he won't, because we'll have got it already.

TITO: He's very understanding.

BEATRICE: (*Alarmed.*) You mean he doesn't understand already?

TITO: Course he understands. You heard me explain the… position to him on the phone. Besides I'm sure he's seen a hundred cases like this –

BEATRICE: Like this?

TITO: He's a gynaecologist.

BEATRICE: The parachute!

She moves, he does not.

TITO: Can we please synchronise our movements?

They commence hobbling across the stage. BEATRICE is in front on all fours, TITO behind on his knees, each must support the other.

BEATRICE: I blame the health club for this. Places like that. Young men with nothing better to do all day than work on their bodies and look for action. All those muscles, all those bodies in tight-fitting clothes, all that perspiration. A poor woman like me was bound to fall for it. I shall not be renewing my membership, I can tell you.

TITO: But it was you who made the first move.

BEATRICE: O! 'She was asking for it, your honour'.

TITO: But you did. Ahhh… !

BEATRICE: And I suppose I'm still asking for it, am I?

TITO: It's the way you move your hips –

BEATRICE: The way I danced till three. No, they can't take you away from me – unfortunately. I'm sorry. I realise that it is completely beyond the bounds of reasonable expectation that you might actually be able to contain yourself. Where's this parachute?

TITO: We're there.

BEATRICE: Not a moment too soon.

BEATRICE opens the door of the closet which is in front of her. BEATRICE pulls out a knapsack. She tries to open it.

TITO: The buckles.

BEATRICE unbuckles it.

Now, the cord.

Silently they unfurl the vast whiteness of the parachute, passing the corners of the boundless ocean of silk from one to the other, and, untangling the strings, the two finally succeed in winding themselves up in a gigantic and shapeless convolvulus of fabric. Pause.

Now the light.

BEATRICE: O God, is it far?

TITO: No.

TITO turns it on. Pause.

BEATRICE: Will he be long, your father?

TITO: Said he was on his away.

BEATRICE: You know, I would have thought that if you had even the slightest inkling that this might happen you could have informed me.

TITO: Firstly, I did not think there was even the

tiniest possibility of this happening. And secondly, it was you gave me the green light.

BEATRICE: Amber at the most.

TITO: It certainly wasn't red.

BEATRICE: Remind me never to catch a ride with you. Again.

TITO: 'From behind' you said. Not much ambiguity in that. It was almost an order.

BEATRICE: That has many interpretations.

TITO: Like what, for instance?

BEATRICE: This is neither the time nor the place.

TITO: Means only one thing in my book.

BEATRICE: You should read more widely.

He shudders and wipes the sweat from his brow.

You're shaking. Why are you shaking? You're at it again. Stop it. Stop it, I said!

TITO: Ahh... !

BEATRICE: You've got unlimited resources.

TITO: He might, but I don't.

BEATRICE: I suppose, in a certain light, it could be seen as flattering.

TITO: You know, it's my first time, like this, I mean. (*Pause.*) Have you ever... you know... before... ?

BEATRICE: (*Reluctantly.*) Only the once.

TITO: Once now or once before?

BEATRICE: Once before! Once before!

TITO: Then you should know what to do.

BEATRICE: It was a long time ago.

TITO: How long?

BEATRICE: When I was young.

TITO: You're still young.

BEATRICE: Forget it, sonny.

TITO: Honest. (*Pause.*) So how was it for you?
Then, I mean.

BEATRICE: It was beautiful.

TITO: How did it end?

BEATRICE: It ended, at least. We emerged, looking
at the stars and went our *separate* ways.

Pause.

TITO: You know, I'm beginning to think you hate me.

BEATRICE: I don't hate you, it just never struck me
that you had it in you.

TITO: What?

BEATRICE: All this. All that.

TITO: I've heard it depends on circumstances.

BEATRICE: Even so, it still strikes me as
physiologically abnormal.

TITO: You'd nothing but praise for me before, now
you're doing me down.

BEATRICE: Without much success, it has to be said.

TITO: You know, I have an idea why this might
have happened.

BEATRICE: Well?

TITO: I don't want to say, in case you take it the wrong way.

BEATRICE: Well, even if I do, I'll pretend I haven't.

TITO: Well, you see...don't you see... ? All of this...

BEATRICE: Yes?

TITO: Well, couldn't all of this mean I might love you?

BEATRICE: Good God! Tell me about your father.

TITO: Don't ignore me.

BEATRICE: Your father's about to arrive, tell me about him. Is he really old, or is that just from your juvenile perspective –

TITO: But I'm telling you I love you. That I might love you, at any rate.

BEATRICE: Is he good-looking?

TITO: He's my dad.

BEATRICE: I see. And your mother?

TITO: I'd prefer not to talk about it.

BEATRICE: Like that, is it?

TITO: It's a very sad story.

BEATRICE: For whom? Him, her or you?

TITO: All three of us.

BEATRICE: Sorry I asked. I've seen enough of your dirty linen for one day, thank you very much.

TITO: (*Manoeuvring under the parachute.*) I said it was sad, not sordid.

BEATRICE: What are you up to now?

TITO: I'm having another go.

BEATRICE: But you said you couldn't.

TITO: It feels a bit better. Talking helps relax me.

BEATRICE: Well, for goodness' sake, let's talk then. Where were we?

TITO: My mother.

He looks stealthily under the parachute.

Hallelujah! I can see it.

BEATRICE: How much?

TITO: Enough to know it's still there.

BEATRICE: Ahh… It's still there, alright, it's coming back for more.

TITO: Please, it might be a turn-on for you –

BEATRICE: A turn on? Aaaah! This is the lowest depths of hell. And, for your information, I do not find the lowest depths of hell a turn-on –

TITO: It's as though it was gripped by an iron fist, dragging me deeper and deeper into… the unknown.

BEATRICE: Maybe you should go with it. See where it takes you –

TITO: I've gone as far into the unknown as I want for one day. You're not the only one who's suffering, you know. I'll give it a tug.

BEATRICE: A short, sharp, shock.

TITO: A short, sharp, shock. I just need a counterbalance.

BEATRICE: (*Holding on to a piece of furniture.*) I'll anchor you. On the count of three; one –

TITO: I'm terribly sorry but it's quite difficult holding it with both hands, if you could take it –

BEATRICE: Listen, if I could take it now I'd have taken it twenty minutes ago. Besides, how am I meant to pull myself forward?

TITO: Well, I'm off-balance too –

BEATRICE: It's still easier for you than it is for me.

TITO: (*Manoeuvring under the parachute.*) I'll try levering it with my thumbs.

BEATRICE laughs.

What's so funny?

BEATRICE: It tickles.

TITO: It's slippy.

BEATRICE: This is an official warning; no more nonsense. One, two…

TITO: God help us.

BEATRICE: The less he knows about this the better.

TITO: You're a believer?

BEATRICE: It's a long story. You?

TITO: Just a figure of speech.

BEATRICE: Listen, the sooner we do this, the sooner we get out.

TITO: Ready when you are.

BEATRICE: One. Two...

TITO: (*Screams.*) Threeeee!!!!

A heave from her, a heave from him, then they both cry in unison.

BEATRICE/TITO: Aahhhhh... !

They collapse painfully. Pause.

BEATRICE: (*Feebly.*) Once, yes, I believed. Unquestioningly. But then the first crack of doubt appeared, and the edifice of my faith – for it was nothing more than an edifice – crumbled completely. It's gone back in again, hasn't it?

TITO: Lock, stock –

BEATRICE: Yes, I'm aware of the barrel too.

TITO: It's the recoil.

BEATRICE: As with a rifle.

TITO: The physics must be similar.

BEATRICE: You're shaking again. You're perspiring too. Please don't perspire.

TITO: I'm sorry, but –

BEATRICE: But what?

TITO: I don't feel very well.

BEATRICE: Right, you may perspire, just don't be sick.

TITO: Not sick like that.

BEATRICE: Well, sick like what then?

TITO: Like I'm having an attack. It's my heart –

BEATRICE: You're too young to have heart problems –

TITO: It's a result of –

BEATRICE: Of what?

TITO: I suffer from… It starts to flutter when –

BEATRICE: Oh come on! When what?

TITO: Claustrophobic situations.

BEATRICE: So?

TITO: Well 'he' seems to suffer from it worse than I do.

The doorbell rings.

(*Recovering rapidly.*) Dad!… That'll be my dad.

BEATRICE: Thank heavens for small mercies.

TITO: Coming, Dad!

BEATRICE: Not again!

TITO: To the door.

BEATRICE: Must we?

The two of them set off with some awkwardness. The doorbell rings again.

TITO: (*Loudly.*) Nearly there, Dad! (*To BEATRICE.*) You know, I always dreamed of the day I'd introduce someone like you to my Dad and say 'Dad, this is my woman.'

BEATRICE: I think, in this instance, that would be stating the obvious.

TITO: What's wrong?

BEATRICE: It's my turn for an attack.

TITO: You're not going to pass out, are you?

BEATRICE: An attack of modesty.

TITO: But it's Dad. He's come to the rescue.

BEATRICE: It's so humiliating.

TITO: Well, it's a bit late for modesty.

BEATRICE: Right, I'll go, but I simply refuse to show my face.

She covers her face with a section of the parachute. Another ring, the pair arrive near the door.

Just to be on the safe side, ask who it is.

TITO: It's him. I recognise his heavy breathing.

He unlocks the door. A final ring.

It's open!

The door opens suddenly and strikes BEATRICE who recoils immediately.

Ahhh...

The pair fall backwards finishing huddled up close to the wall. TOBIA peers in.

TOBIA: Hello! Anybody at – There you are. Very good. Yes. Right. What's all this then? Bit out of our depth, are we? Bit off more than we can chew, have we? I see.

TITO: Dad, please, there's tension enough –

TOBIA moves around the room at speed. He throws his coat in one corner, his bag in another, and his hat in yet another. In his hand he holds a medical instrument; the retractor.

TOBIA: Tension? Tension? What's there to be tense about. Good Lord, tension! It's hardly the end of the world is it? Have no fear, have no fear your father is here. You should learn to relax, that's what you should do instead of going round making mountains out of molehills, making sows ears out of silk purses, and all that. We'll soon have you out of your little pickle. Good Lord, I must say, when you rang and told me, I must say, I did laugh. (*He laughs.*) I must say, yes, I laughed. Well, it was actually as I was leaving and I met Fredo on the stairs – Fredo's just been elected president of the club, you know – and it was as I was telling him that I began to see the funny side of it. It was at that point I began to laugh, to be precise. And he said to me: 'What's up, Doc?' And I said: 'My son's up, that's what.' 'Your little Tito stuck up the Kyber Pass? I don't believe it,' he said. So I waved my retractor under his nose, and he laughed and he said: 'What's that for? Curling your moustache?' 'That,' I said, 'is for uncorking my son.' (*He laughs.*) That's why I was delayed. Peppe, the caretaker, was there too and he wanted to know the whole story. And Mrs Rossi. And her twins. Yes, I really did begin to see the funny side. (*He laughs.*)

BEATRICE: The very soul of discretion.

TITO: Did you have to tell Peppe and Mrs Rossi and the twins as well?

TOBIA: Are these the prints Aunt Gianna gave you? Very good, very nice, I'm sure. And the drinks trolley you brought over from the house? Haven't you set it up yet? And speaking of Aunt Gianna; don't forget dinner in her house, tomorrow.

BEATRICE: I'd prefer not to have to attend as well.

TOBIA: Good Lord, looks as though a bomb hit the place! There was some hanky-panky going on here! (*Professional tone.*) Right. Bon, fun's over, to work.

Goes to BEATRICE, hand outstretched.

First of all, let me –

TITO: I think it would be more appropriate to look for a way to resolve the present situation. She's a little anxious. Modesty.

TOBIA: Not shared, obviously.

TOBIA takes off his jacket, he rolls up his shirt sleeves. With his back to the other two, he sets about testing his retractor.

BEATRICE: What's he up to now?

TITO: Testing his equipment.

BEATRICE: Equipment?

TITO: For the operation.

BEATRICE: Operation!

BEATRICE, making sure TOBIA cannot see her, sticks her head out from under the parachute.

What's that?

TITO: A retractor. He designed it himself. Cost an arm and a leg. Top German technology. Had it manufactured in Bonn. We had to live on bread and water for two months to pay for it.

TOBIA: (*Without turning round.*) Please! The time for fun is over. We must get down to business.

TOBIA turns around. BEATRICE, quick as lightening hides her head under the cover. TOBIA approaches the pair of them.

TITO: It's not… going to hurt, is it Dad?

TOBIA: What doesn't kill you makes you stronger.

He discretely raises a section of the parachute.

BEATRICE: There's a draft.

TOBIA: Would you have me work in a vacuum?

TITO: Ahh!

TOBIA: Sore?

TITO: A bit.

TOBIA: You must endure the hardship.

BEATRICE: Perhaps, but I refuse to endure the *double entendres* as well!

TOBIA: I beg your pardon.

BEATRICE: Ahhh!

TOBIA: (*To BEATRICE.*) Sore?

BEATRICE: No, I thought you might care to inspect my tonsils while you were at it!

TOBIA: Your tonsils? Good Lord, this is worse than I thought.

BEATRICE: Will you please just hurry up.

TOBIA: (*Perplexed.*) It is a difficult case. Yes. A difficult case alright. It's deadlock.

BEATRICE: What do you mean?

TOBIA: (*Replacing his retractor.*) A chain reaction. He swells, you contract. The contraction brings on the swelling, the swelling causes contraction. A vicious circle, a sum to infinity… stalemate.

TITO: And so?

TOBIA: We must outsmart it.

BEATRICE: How?

TOBIA: Exactly. I must have a think.

He departs for the inside room. Pause.

BEATRICE: Well? Have you thought about enough, yet?

TITO: He's gone.

BEATRICE: (*Uncovering her face.*) Where?

TITO: The bedroom.

BEATRICE: But not 'gone' gone?

TITO: No. He's in there. Thinking. The heavy breathing. Listen.

BEATRICE: I knew he wouldn't be able to help. You could have told me your father was stark raving mad.

TITO: He's not mad, he's just a bit eccentric.

BEATRICE: He's completely insane.

TITO: You don't know him.

BEATRICE: He's aroused. I can tell. He's not thinking. He's gone inside to masturbate.

TITO: My father does not masturbate.

BEATRICE: I saw. That's what he's up to, believe you me.

TITO: What could you see from there?

BEATRICE: I saw enough.

TITO: He's coming back, and he was not masturbating. He's a doctor.

BEATRICE turns to hide herself. TOBIA returns.

TOBIA: Right. Yes. There we are.

BEATRICE: Had a good think?

He goes to his bag and opens it. He pulls out a syringe and some phials. During the following dialogue he fills the syringe with a mixture of doses taken from various phials.

TOBIA: You know it's not every doctor would have such respect for his patients' feelings. I could, if I so chose, exercise the letter of the law and insist your friend reveal her identity. Yes. What do you think of that, Madame?

BEATRICE: First remove your son from my rectum, then I'll remove the parachute.

TOBIA: (*Checking.*) Parachute? Good God, a parachute. Did you not have anything else to cover yourselves with?

TITO: She said my sheets were filthy.

TOBIA: And are they?

BEATRICE: See for yourself.

TOBIA: (*Smacking TITO.*) You filthy pig! You should be ashamed of yourself. You're an embarrassment to your father. What will people think? That you never had a father? That no one slaved night and day so that you could be brought up in a sanitary environment? The years of struggle I endured for you, and all to hear that your sheets are filthy. What kind of host are you? What kind of hospitality do you call this? What will people think? I'll tell you what they'll think. They'll think it's his parents' fault, that's what they'll think. (*To BEATRICE.*) I hope that's not what you think, Madame. Please say that's not what you think.

BEATRICE: My first thought.

TOBIA: (*Another smack.*) See?! That's what she thinks. Her very first thought, you... you good-for-nothing. Haven't I told you that if you won't give them to me to wash, you could always take them to the launderette. I even offered to pay.

TITO: I was going to get them washed tomorrow.

TOBIA: Tomorrow! Tomorrow! Always tomorrow! You... good-for-nothing. Still sore?

TITO: (*Sullenly.*) Same.

TOBIA: You must excuse me, I give my son a calculated smack every now and then. It's the only way of getting through, sometimes. He'd be even worse if I didn't. Yes. A smack every now and then never hurt anyone.

TITO: But it did hurt.

TOBIA: Typical, making me appear the villain. Are you never done embarrassing me? Tell her you'd be the worse for not having the odd smack.

TITO: Leave it out, Dad.

TOBIA: What? Are you going to do what your father says, or must I beat it out of you? Tell her. Tell her you'd suffer for not having the odd smack.

TITO: Sometimes you get on my wick, you know that, Dad.

BEATRICE: Well, let him get on it so long as I get off it.

TOBIA gives him another smack.

TOBIA: And there's more where that came from.

BEATRICE: For the love of God, say it. The reverberations are agony.

TITO: (*Defeated.*) I would suffer.

BEATRICE: Thank God.

TOBIA: That wasn't so bad, was it? Right. Yes. Now. Where were we?

BEATRICE: Back where we started.

TOBIA: Yes. Yes. That's it. Time to get down to business. Pull here.

TITO: Why?

TOBIA: I have to give you an injection.

BEATRICE: What injection?

TOBIA: To aid detumescence.

TITO: Christ, not an injection!

BEATRICE: If you continue to take the Lord's name, I'll... I'll... I'll not stand for it! Do you hear me? I'll not stand for it!

TOBIA: Has he been taking the Lord's name? Have you been taking the Lord's name? You have been taking the Lord's name. He has been taking the Lord's name, hasn't he?

TITO: It's only natural. The throes of passion, and all that.

TOBIA: You took the Lord's name in the throes of passion?!

TITO: It just came out.

BEATRICE: Please forget it. It was only natural, like he said. Perhaps a drink might relax you? Might relax us all.

TOBIA: Not content with filthy sheets, you must stoop to taking the Lord's name. Thou shalt not take the Lord's name, thou shalt not –

BEATRICE: It's alright. It hurt no one –

TITO: I'm sorry, Dad –

TOBIA: 'Dad' 'Dad'! You only think of your dad when you're in trouble. It's only then you remember you have a father. But more often than not, your dad is just a pain in the backside.

TOBIA viciously jabs the needle into TITO's backside.

TITO: Ahh!

BEATRICE: Ahhh!

TOBIA: And now, all we can do is wait till it gets round your system. It's a fair old dose.

He whips his eye immodestly under the parachute.

(*Betraying a certain euphoria.*) It's like a large fish, skewered on a harpoon. I've never seen anything like it! (*Patting TITO's head.*) You know, when all's said and done, it does make an old man proud –

BEATRICE: (*Whimpering.*) The draft!

TOBIA: (*Covering them.*) You must excuse me, Madame. The little bursts of pride. But a father and a son... what can one say?

BEATRICE: One could say something that might not cause offence.

TOBIA: Now she's insulting my manners when she doesn't even have the politeness to show her face.

BEATRICE: This is getting us nowhere. Please, let's change the subject.

TITO: (*Massaging his rear.*) It's burning.

TOBIA: Good.

TITO: But it's burning really badly.

BEATRICE: Divine retribution.

TOBIA: A good, strong dose was called for.

TITO: Are you sure it wasn't too much?

TOBIA: Will you stop interrupting me? I would like to talk to your friend. (*To BEATRICE.*) We were talking about my little fits of pride, were we not? What you don't understand is that not only am I a doctor, I am also a father. A doctor diagnoses then treats – coldly, clinically, without passion – but a father – ? Blood is not water, it's oil, it's a highly flammable substance, it bursts into flames at the merest spark, it exults –

BEATRICE: Blood tears you apart.

TOBIA: No, blood is the adhesive that glues –

BEATRICE: I thought it was oil that bursts into flames –

TOBIA: It's a highly flammable oil-based adhesive. You're a woman, a mother, maybe, and mothers, as you know –

BEATRICE: Excuse me, I think we have pursued this line of conversation far enough.

TOBIA: I beg your pardon?

BEATRICE: No more.

TOBIA: I was only speaking hypothetically.

BEATRICE: Well, no more.

TOBIA: Well, fathers then, am I permitted to talk about fathers?

BEATRICE: Fathers are permissible.

TOBIA: Well, a father sees things in his son, things which a mother – I mean mothers in general – could never understand, at least in some matters. Between men there is an understanding, understanding that comes from being on the same pole-vaulting team as each other, so to speak. This is the source of my pride.

BEATRICE: If you do not wish to completely humiliate me, then would you please desist from the present line of conversation.

TOBIA: Humiliate you?

BEATRICE: Don't come the innocent!

TOBIA: The innocent?

BEATRICE: You are a male chauvinist –

TOBIA: I am a father. A father! That's what I am. A father who cannot and should not dilute his joy on finding that his son, his only son, the continuation of my DNA in this world, proves that he has the capability to hold high the name he has inherited.

BEATRICE: You're over-excitable, that's what you are –

TOBIA: Why shouldn't I get excited. You've seen them, 'the yoofs of today'. No direction, no ambition, unwilling to shoulder any responsibility. Maybe you think it's easy to make something of your son –

BEATRICE: What son? I have no son!

TOBIA: One's son. A son. Sons in general. You think it's easy, don't you? Well let me tell you, it's not. So when I see that he's not some layabout lout like the rest of them, but someone who has got up off his *derrière* and taken arms against a sea of sloth and, like a young David, hurled himself into battle with Goliath without fear –

BEATRICE: My *derrière* is not Goliath!

TOBIA: I meant it metaphorically.

BEATRICE: Well, now he's floored me, let him pick up his sling and scram.

TOBIA: And you know, between ourselves, I had actually feared the worst –

TITO: Dad, please don't bring that up again –

TOBIA: Why not, now that you've proved yourself to be a man? I'm not embarrassed, I'm not afraid to apologise for my previous misgivings. I feared that he'd end up like Richie Spaccamenta – filthy Richie – a school acquaintance of his.

BEATRICE: It was just a phase, I'm sure. They all go through phases, I'm told.

TOBIA: That's it. And adolescence; what a phase! They're neither fish nor fowl, bird nor beast. A no-man's-land where any one of a hundred things can go wrong and a poor father can do nothing but wait.

TITO: The only thing I ever did with Richie was my homework.

TOBIA: You did more than that. You used to measure it.

BEATRICE: But that's normal.

TITO: Try telling him that.

TOBIA: It is normal to measure it with a tape-measure. God knows how many tape-measures I gave him! Or a ruler. But no, they had to use their hands. In fact his hand. (*Takes TITO by the wrist.*) This very hand did for both of them.

TITO: But we needed a yardstick.

TOBIA: Well, it's all water under the bridge now. This is an altogether different ball game. My son is a lady-killer!

BEATRICE: I hope you are speaking metaphorically again.

TITO yawns.

TOBIA: Put your hand over your mouth, you good-for-nothing lout!

TITO: It's the injection.

TOBIA: It's relaxing him. Shows it's working.

BEATRICE: He just came again.

TOBIA: O.

TITO: It happens without me noticing anymore.

BEATRICE: I'm worn out. It's unbearable.

TOBIA: (*Giving TITO a friendly cuff on the cheek.*) And this the same rapscallion who'd never let himself be seen naked, not even by his own father.

BEATRICE: I'm worn out by the two of you.

TOBIA: By us both? But he's done it all on his own, that's the point.

BEATRICE: Go away! Just go away all of you! Go on! Scram!

TITO: Please, you're doing me an injury.

BEATRICE: (*Beside herself.*) Let me get this straight
with you – with both of you – before your
arrival I would have sooner died than expose
myself like this in a hospital; the paramedics,
the orderlies, the bloody doctors. I can just
imagine their snide sniggering. What a *butt* for
all their jokes. But this ordeal, which I must now
endure, is worse, much worse. I'd rather be dead.
I don't care any more. I really don't. We've
plumbed the depths, so let's go the whole hog –
what does it matter anymore? – the ridicule of
the world. I'm worn out, I tell you. I'm a broken
woman and you are here to finish me off. Fate,
do your damnedest! (*She sobs, then picks it up again.*)
Must I be exposed for all the world to see with
my knickers round my ankles? So be it. And
you, Lord God Almighty, fat lot of good you
are. Fat lot of good you've ever been. God
forgive me. But only suffering piled on suffering.
The same old story. Well so be it. Bring it on.
The fat lady and all. Let her start singing, for
the love of God. Perhaps then and only then will
I be able to redeem this life in which so many
brief pleasures have been more than balanced
by a few, but resounding calamities. What am
I telling you two all this for? For the love of
God, let's put an end to this. I find your
conversation more humiliating than the actual
situation. So, we made a mistake. I made a
mistake. I consented to sodomy. According to
some this forever bars me from the kingdom of
heaven. I have committed a sin, one which I had
already committed in my youth. And my only
justification can be that I was carried away by
the all too human desire to return, however
vainly, to that day long gone when a great love

stirred – yes, before you say it – stirred my very
bowels and since that day, since that day, the
deluge –

TITO yawns spectacularly, then comes.

Well, that was the most enjoyable of my sins.
I felt shame, but – by God – did I enjoy it. But
the past doesn't return. Just look at this glorious
attempt to recapture it. Pathetic. I am pathetic.
And you, don't think you're without blame. You
two are accomplices to my damnation, and if
I cover my face, it's not to hide mine, but to
avoid seeing yours. That's why I'm begging you,
let's get out of here.

TITO: Aaaaooooo… !

BEATRICE: Take me wherever you want; to a
public square, put me on television, afternoon
television even, I don't care… but please, put an
end to this torture. First, you are a quack and
second, you are evil-minded. (*She cries. She rallies.*)
Excuse me Tito, I understand he's your father,
and perhaps you are used to looking at him
through rose-tinted glasses, but believe me, I've
seen a few evil-minded quacks in my time and
he takes the biscuit. Please, call an ambulance,
call an ambulance, for pity's sake.

TITO: Mrs Riccobono, please, everything will be
alright.

TOBIA: (*To TITO.*) So, she's married –

*TITO indicates to keep quiet. TOBIA fails to mask an expression of
satisfaction.*

Let her get it off her chest. It's better. It might
even help her relax and facilitate your release.

You were right. Too much tension, far too much tension.

BEATRICE continues to cry.

TITO: Dad, it's happening again –

BEATRICE: Must you always broadcast it?

TITO: My heart.

BEATRICE: O, that.

TOBIA: Your grandfather was the same, during the bombardment.

TITO: What's Grandpa got to do with this?

BEATRICE: Or the bombardment. What the hell does the bombardment have to do with it? (*Pause.*) Apart from the blindingly obvious –

TOBIA: Similar reaction. He was family. (*Reassuring BEATRICE.*) You certainly have quite a tongue on you. Like a scalpel; slash, slash, slash. You should try to stay calm. Quite apart from anything else, I find it quite hurtful, your aspersions as to my professional abilities. Do you think, just because we are specialists, we are immune from being hurt? Do you think we have no feelings? We are human. Though I suppose we at the front line of research should expect this sort of thing. We should draw strength from them. What doesn't kill you, and all that.

He takes a wallet out of an inside pocket and takes out some photographs.

TITO: Dad no – !

TOBIA: (*To BEATRICE.*) If I've, you know, upset you, by my bedside-manner, I didn't mean to. It wasn't my intention. I did it out of love –

TITO: But Dad – !

TOBIA: Shut up, you. (*To BEATRICE.*) Paternal love. And love is blind, they say. And perhaps that blinded me to the sensitive nature of your position. I had to raise him alone, you know. I don't resent it, not a bit. He was my son, my blood –

He places the photograph under the edge of the parachute which covers BEATRICE's head.

Look, his first day at school.

TITO: Oh, please – !

BEATRICE, while continuing to cry, is constrained to look. Eventually the sobs subside.

TOBIA: Well, what do you think?

BEATRICE: Really quite sweet. (*Brief pause.*) His hair's a bit long –

TOBIA: Here he is with the under-twelves. He's number five.

TITO: I gave up before secondary school!

BEATRICE: And this one?

TOBIA: That's Richie. Beside him.

BEATRICE: The one holding his hand?

TOBIA: Yes.

BEATRICE: He was quite a charming little boy, Tito.

TOBIA: Yes! Yes, he was. (*Giving her a third photograph.*) This one's us on holiday in Valsugana. That's me.

BEATRICE: (*Taking the photo, very interested.*) Ah, Valsugana –

TOBIA: Been there?

BEATRICE: When I was young.

> *BEATRICE looks at it. A few seconds silence, then she lets a scream; she pulls her head out from under the parachute.*

You!

TOBIA: Ah!

BEATRICE: Tobia!

TOBIA: Beatrice!

BEATRICE: Tobia Galeazzi!

TOBIA: Beatrice Pastrengo!

BEATRICE: I've finally found you, you shit!

TITO: Aaaah... (*Pause.*) Will someone please explain – ?

> *End of Act One.*

ACT TWO

Moments later. BEATRICE no longer needs to hide. A pause.

TITO: Why did she call you a shit, Dad?

TOBIA: Yes, well, exactly. Why did you call me a shit, Beatrice? After all, it's over – Good Lord – over twenty years since we last saw each other. Our last year in school –

BEATRICE: Who cares when it was? You shit from hell?

Pause.

TITO: And how come you know Mrs Riccobono, Dad?

TOBIA: Riccobono indeed! I look forward to hearing that little story. You were always inclined toward fantasies. 'Me? Marry? Never!' It must have been Mr Riccobono's spiritual passion which consumed her. 'I give to my soul, that which I deny my flesh.'

BEATRICE: You're talking of things long buried.

TITO: Well, maybe you two should bury the hatchet. (*Pause.*) It's funny, the way the most everyday expressions can take on altogether different meanings.

Pause.

BEATRICE: There is no hatchet to bury!

TOBIA: There was.

BEATRICE: I don't know what you're talking about.

TOBIA: I'm talking about us! Us in our heyday –

BEATRICE: There was no us. There was no heyday.

TOBIA: No us? No heyday? Who was it clutched your hand tight to his breast as we sat on the wrought iron bench under the summer sun –

BEATRICE: I can't hear you. My hands are over my ears and I can't hear you. So stop it.

She blocks her ears.

TITO: You were in the same class? What a coincidence!

BEATRICE: Dredging up your own disgrace, not mine. That's all you're doing. You're rotten. Rotten to your very core.

TOBIA: What about you?

TITO: (*Yawning.*) That stuff you gave me, Dad, it's making me very sleepy.

TOBIA: We were both there, still trembling from the night of passion stolen from under the beady eye of Father Gosetti during that sleepless week-long retreat in Valsugana –

TITO: Strange; if I yawn – (*He yawns.*) – I get turned on. Ahhh! …

TOBIA: I noticed Valsugana rang a bell for you.

BEATRICE: Did you? And did you also notice perchance, that it was there you ruined my life!

TOBIA: We'd been together since fourth year –

BEATRICE: I wasn't in the fourth year, I came from the technical college.

TOBIA: Well, from the fifth then.

TITO: (*Wrestling a yawn.*) I reckon you put the wrong part of me to sleep.

TOBIA: (*Still to BEATRICE.*) And on that last night of the holiday, a bit tipsy –

BEATRICE: That's why I did it. The only reason –

TOBIA: – and you whispered in my ear: 'Take me!'

TITO submits to his yawning with obvious consequences, after which he arranges a cushion on BEATRICE's back so he can rest his head.

BEATRICE: 'Take me!'; those two words have so many interpretations. And yet they've given you the alibi you've needed ever since.

TOBIA: So many interpretations? There's only one in my book.

BEATRICE: Your family should join a book club.

TOBIA: But you consented, carried away with a love that for five years –

BEATRICE: Four.

TOBIA: Four then – a love whose every twist and turn was detailed in my tortured verses – somewhat naively, perhaps – but sincere, nevertheless. I filled jotters full of the damned things.

BEATRICE: Don't think this will get you off the hook. You shit!

TOBIA: What hook? Was it not you, that summer morning, on the wrought iron bench, under the sun, as we revised our Ancient History, was it not you who, when I said 'Marry me! Marry me! Marry me!' you who said 'No! No! No!' like John the Baptist in his hole.

BEATRICE: I don't remember him falling asleep.

TITO: (*Distantly.*) I'm still here. Ahhh…

TOBIA: Don't try to get out of it.

BEATRICE: Believe me, if I could get out of it, I would.

TOBIA: You had loftier aspirations!

BEATRICE: Stop it.

TOBIA: To join the Marcellines, I do recall.

BEATRICE: I did join the Marcellines –

TOBIA: Is that so? And is this the convent habit, then?

BEATRICE: I kicked the convent habit. And, ever since, I've sunk further and further into the... the quagmire.

TOBIA: 'I can't do it. The Lord has called me. I will place my life in his hands.' I remember it like it was yesterday. 'As for our night of sin, it is a black pearl I must bear in the shell of my body.'

BEATRICE: Your sin was greater than mine.

TOBIA: What sin? To give you the love you asked of me?

BEATRICE: To give me a son.

Silence, then TOBIA bursts out laughing.

TOBIA: Haha, I do believe you've finally snapped. Flipped. Gone entirely round the twist. A son? Me? Me and you?

BEATRICE: You dare deny it, you bastard!? Or should I say you dare to deny *your* bastard, you bastard? How can you pretend you didn't know?

TITO: (*Starting.*) I've a little brother? (*Yawns.*)
    Ahhh… !

TOBIA: I've told you before, put your hand over
    your mouth when you yawn.

BEATRICE: (*Throwing the cushion off her back.*) You're a
    fine one to tell people how they should and
    should not behave, you bastard!

TOBIA: The language of a Marcelline.

BEATRICE: For some time now I have been
    something other than what I was, or what I strove
    and failed to be.

TOBIA: That, my dear lady, is all too apparent.

BEATRICE: Then why the interrogation?

TOBIA: You're asking me? You? When you know that
    since that day on the wrought iron bench my heart
    has remained broken, irrevocably broken, and the
    reason it has remained irrevocably broken, is you.

BEATRICE: Your heart! What about my life? Yes,
    we parted and went our separate ways. And yes,
    I didn't search for you exactly, but in that way
    that a woman doesn't search, that is, in the
    secret hope of being found. I can admit it now.
    It wasn't clear to me then, but now, now I am
    prepared to admit that my feelings concerning
    our separation were mixed.

TITO: (*Thinking.*) A step-brother! That makes you a
    kind of aunty –

TOBIA: (*Smacking him.*) Don't interrupt. I've told
    you a hundred times –

BEATRICE: But at that stage I was still intent on
    taking my vows. I joined an enclosed order.

Alone, with only the four walls for company.
But, as time passed, my desires and confusion
gradually turned to a spiritual piety. I became
the Abbess's favourite. Saintly Beatrice, the
pearl of the convent. They had great hopes for
me and I went about my duties with bowed head
and due solemnity. But all the while, like some
black advent, the seed of your foul offspring
took root in my belly.

TOBIA: You've lost me.

BEATRICE: Damn you! Damn you! How can I begin
to describe to you the horror, the anguish, the
terror of my nights and days?

TOBIA: Are you trying to trap me? Because if this
is a trap –

BEATRICE: You ignorant bloody bastard! You
haven't changed –

TOBIA: I apologise. I should at least hear out your
little story.

BEATRICE: In my torment, I retained one single,
solitary hope: Tobia! Tobia! Tobia! But it was
soon noticed that my belly was growing. My
private despair soon became public gossip. A
friend of mine – a real friend of mine – said to
me: 'Tobia? I know where he is.'

TOBIA: And which friend might that be?

BEATRICE: 'He's abroad, in Switzerland.'

TOBIA: That's true. I too was in a religious
institution. But for different reasons. On retreat
in Canton Ticino.

BEATRICE: 'Calm down, Beatrice, I'll get hold of
him. I'll let him know – '

TOBIA: I never heard from anyone.

BEATRICE: You liar!

TITO: Christ Dad, this is some story –

TOBIA: (*Smacking him.*) I've told you before, do not take the Lord's name.

BEATRICE: 'He doesn't want to know. He never wants to hear from you again.' Etcetera, etcetera. That is exactly what a good friend of yours told me. I remember like it was yesterday.

TOBIA: As I said, I would be extremely grateful to know who this 'good' friend was.

BEATRICE: And with that, my last hope gone, my world collapsed. My family threatened to throw me out of my home, just like I'd been thrown out of the convent. I was on the point of terminating... But I didn't want to.

TOBIA: You shouldn't have had to, if you didn't want to.

BEATRICE: Easy for you to say that.

TOBIA: Of course, because it has nothing to do with me.

BEATRICE: But it has to do with your son. I didn't murder your son, but I still had to pay the heaviest price a mother can pay.

TOBIA: I beg your pardon, but if what you say really did happen – about your pregnancy and this so-called 'friend' who told me of your predicament – it would have been the happiest day of my life.

BEATRICE: Lies! Lies! Lies! Men all over, for you!

TOBIA: Believe me, Beatrice. This story makes me feel quite weak at the knees.

TITO: What do you mean, Dad?

BEATRICE: It means he doesn't know which way to run.

TOBIA: You've had your say, let me have mine.

TITO: Dad! Dad! Something's happening –

TOBIA: (*Retrieving his retractor.*) Right. Yes. First I must examine him, then I'll explain.

He fusses between them with his instruments.

BEATRICE: I'm glad to see that you have finally realised that it's not the conversation that has been detaining us –

TITO: Christ, you're crucifying me!

Pause.

TOBIA: Perhaps we should wait.

TITO: Please, let's wait.

TOBIA: And while we wait, we can see how my side matches up to hers.

TITO: You've completely crushed it.

BEATRICE: I should be so lucky.

TOBIA: (*To BEATRICE.*) For a start, then: do you remember what was the first thing I said to you that night?

BEATRICE: When?

TOBIA: That night! That night! That 'night of sin'!

BEATRICE: Yes, I do.

TOBIA: And what was it?

BEATRICE: I embarrassed to say it, in front of...

TOBIA: What, him? Why on earth would you be embarrassed to say it in front of him?

BEATRICE: Well then, if you insist; 'from behind'.

TOBIA: I beg your pardon?

BEATRICE: That was it.

TOBIA: But what?

BEATRICE: The first thing you said to me.

TOBIA: Me?

BEATRICE: Yes you, you filthy pig!

TOBIA: From behind?

BEATRICE: Now come on!

TITO: That's it.

TOBIA: What is 'it'?

TITO: That was the first thing she said to me too.

TOBIA: Her?

TITO: Yup.

TOBIA: From behind?

TITO: Well, not exactly.

TOBIA: What then?

TITO: 'Roll me over.' That was it. 'Roll me over and do it from behind.'

TOBIA: The first thing?

TITO: She came straight out with it.

BEATRICE: Something impelled me.

TOBIA: But it wasn't the first thing I said to her.

BEATRICE: It was the first and the last thing that you said to me.

TOBIA: I beg your pardon, but it was neither the first nor the last thing I said to you. I never said it to you.

BEATRICE: What did you say to me then?

TOBIA: Don't worry, I said, I have a problem of diminishing returns.

BEATRICE: I've no idea what you mean.

TOBIA: Of course you do, because that was the first thing I said to you, that night.

BEATRICE: Well if that is the case, if you have this problem, as you say, what about Tito?

TOBIA: Exactly.

BEATRICE: Exactly.

Pause.

TOBIA: I have always had this problem.

BEATRICE: Always?

TOBIA: Some might see it as quite a convenient 'problem'. It can save one a lot of problems, this problem of mine. One can sow one's oats far and wide without having to worry about harvesting, so to speak. Though the benefits didn't quite strike me when they discovered it at my military service medical –

BEATRICE: Excuse me, but I'm completely at a loss –

TOBIA: It's quite simple –

BEATRICE: But Tito. Here. Larger than bloody life.

TOBIA: Well, yes, medical science and all that. Great strides forward in, you know, these areas, and all that.

BEATRICE: Okay Tito, perhaps, but what about Costatino?

TOBIA: Costatino who?

BEATRICE: My baby. Your son.

TITO: My brother!

TOBIA: Not my doing, I'm afraid.

BEATRICE: Do you deny that it was my doing as well?

TOBIA: Your doing is your own affair. Or was your own affair, I should say. I have manners enough not to press you for an explanation on that score.

BEATRICE: But not quite manners enough not to doubt me.

TOBIA: Doubt you? I have no doubts. I take your word for it; you had a son by someone else.

BEATRICE: But if I went straight from your bed to my bed at the convent –

TOBIA: It might have been my bed, but it most certainly was not me.

BEATRICE: But what about what you said that night?

TOBIA: I laid the case before you and you said: 'Right, if there are no risks, let's get down to business!'

BEATRICE: You're mad. You're completely mad.

TOBIA: I remember as though it were yesterday.

BEATRICE: You said one thing and one thing only, and you repeated it all night: 'From behind.'

TITO: Like father like son, eh Dad? (*He yawns.*) Ahhh…

TOBIA: But why would I have said 'from behind' to you?

BEATRICE: That's all you said to me.

TOBIA: Perhaps there was a timid reconnaissance of the posterior region, but if there was, which I don't recall, it came about in the general course of things. As for specifically requesting –

BEATRICE: Timid reconnaissance? You took me anally –

TOBIA: Anally? You must be joking. Vaginally, I took you vaginally.

BEATRICE: Only once vaginally. You forced it on me. I was afraid. And Lord God, I was right to be afraid –

TOBIA: But I swear I only took you vaginally.

BEATRICE: No, you *also* took me vaginally.

TOBIA: But never anally.

BEATRICE: Anally! Anally! Almost entirely anally.

TOBIA: Beatrice, please, I swear to you, you are mistaken!

BEATRICE: You'd deny your own mother.

TOBIA: That night, I never, ever took you anally.

BEATRICE: When then?

TOBIA: Never! Never ever!

BEATRICE: And does this method of yours for denying the existence of entities which patently exist extend to, I don't know, Milan or the Trans-Siberian Railway?

TITO: Dad, if Mrs Riccobono insists –

TOBIA: But she's saying anally –

BEATRICE: Like I said, once, calamitously, vaginally as well.

TOBIA: But I've told you; only vaginally. Twice vaginally.

BEATRICE: Once vaginally and more than ten times anally!

TITO: Us; once anally. All in.

BEATRICE: (*To TOBIA.*) Face facts.

TOBIA: You face facts.

BEATRICE: The incident which you refuse to remember happens to be the formulating incident of my life, and the one hope I have always clung to is that it was as good for you as it was for me –

TOBIA: But Beatrice, darling, you must believe me when I say that it was. It was as good for me, but as you insist, you know, anally –

BEATRICE: Well I reassert it, anally, anally, anally. You reinserted it enough.

TOBIA: And you don't remember the two times –

BEATRICE: I remember the one. How could I forget?

TOBIA: They weren't completely pathetic attempts.

BEATRICE: Pathetic, no. But fatal, yes.

TOBIA: (*Perplexed.*) Once vaginally and ten times anally?

BEATRICE: More than ten –

TOBIA: More than ten?

BEATRICE: At the very least.

TOBIA: But how could I? A man knows his own limits, and I – Good God, at least ten times – it's completely beyond me!

BEATRICE: These days, perhaps, but not in those.

TOBIA: But who could possibly… ?

BEATRICE: You could, obviously.

TOBIA: That's very kind of you to say, but I'm afraid it's for something I didn't do.

BEATRICE: You liar.

TOBIA: Anally, never, before or since.

BEATRICE: Me neither. After you, I never did it again.

TOBIA: Now you are lying.

BEATRICE: I'm not.

TITO: Can you deny me?

BEATRICE: Until today, I mean. When I saw him in the gym, something told me 'You must'. I admit, I'm no saint. I've had others, a few, but with them I only ever did it, you know –

TOBIA: Vaginally?

BEATRICE: Not to put too fine a point on it, yes. But today, some kind of fateful, or was it fatal, desire –

TOBIA: But more than ten times?

TITO: It's not impossible, Dad. Without much effort even I must have clocked up twenty or so –

TOBIA: No. I'm sorry. I'm afraid, whatever you say, I just cannot claim paternity of this... Costatino.

BEATRICE: As soon as the question of paternity arises, you're in absolute denial. Typical. It's only because you know you can get away with it. All because of that...(*She gestures.*)

TOBIA: That what?

BEATRICE: That! Down there! Because of that battering ram of yours.

TOBIA: Of mine!?

BEATRICE: Now I understand that sudden, inexplicable desire that came over me at the gym. (*Indicates her heart.*) Like an attack, here.

TOBIA: There?

BEATRICE: Here, there and everywhere.

TITO: You should have been there, Dad, I thought I might have to chat her a bit up or something, but she just says it straight out: 'My place is out, is yours far?' (*He yawns.*) Aaaah...

TOBIA: (*Repeats dumbfounded.*) Anally? Ten times?

BEATRICE: At least. At least ten, if not more.

TOBIA: But a battering ram?

BEATRICE: Your primitive instrument of war.

TITO: So that's why you used to always look at me in the bath. You were hoping I'd grow up to be the man that you were. Ah, Dad –

TOBIA, without a word, and with an air of defeat, undoes his trousers.

TOBIA: (*To TITO.*) Right. You, turn away. And no smart alec remarks.

TITO reluctantly averts his gaze. TOBIA, back to the audience, drops his trousers in front of BEATRICE.

Does this strike you as a battering ram?

Silence.

TITO: What? What is it?

BEATRICE: It looks like a penis, only smaller.

End of Act Two.

ACT THREE

A few minutes have elapsed between Acts Two and Three. TOBIA is bustling around the kitchen area.

TOBIA: (*Bringing a cup of coffee to TITO.*) Here's the coffee. Let's hope it wakes you up a bit. (*To BEATRICE.*) Would you care for some, Madame?

BEATRICE shakes her head.

There's plenty. It's no bother. And there's some panetone. A slice of panetone anyone? Keep us going. Keep the wolf from the door. Keep smiling through... Good God, what am I saying?

TOBIA hands around coffees and slices of panetone on sideplates. He has delicately arranged the plates with napkins and tiny cake forks. The three of them drink. BEATRICE does not touch her cake. TITO wolfs his down. TOBIA picks at his. Pause.

You do not care for your panetone, Madame?

BEATRICE: How could I eat panetone at a time like this? And do you think we could drop the formality?

TOBIA: You must excuse me, but I still don't feel it is appropriate given that we are not as familiar with each other as I had previously thought us to be.

He drinks. Pause. Drinks again. TITO blows on his coffee to cool it. BEATRICE places her empty cup on the floor.

Here, let me take care of it. I'll leave the panetone, in case you feel a bit peckish later.

BEATRICE: How long do you expect me to be in this position?

TOBIA: You should eat. Sustain yourself. Be prepared for all eventualities.

He takes the cup away.

TITO: Leave the cups, Dad. I'll wash them up later.

TOBIA sits on the edge of his chair. He sips his coffee. He looks fixedly in front of him. Pause.

TOBIA: Right. I'll give it another short while, and if affairs haven't improved by then, we'll have to consult a specialist.

BEATRICE: I thought you were a specialist.

TITO: Me too.

TOBIA takes a gulp.

TOBIA: I am. I was. But this is an altogether different kettle of fish.

BEATRICE: Please!

TOBIA: It appears to be quite cemented in, Madame.

BEATRICE: I told you he wasn't up to it from the start.

TOBIA: Please, Madame! The conversation concerned my abilities in the area of medical science.

BEATRICE: But how long will we have to wait?

TITO: (*Weakly.*) Ahhh…

TOBIA: So we didn't do it – together, I mean – that night. It wasn't me.

BEATRICE: So it would seem.

TOBIA: Someone else. But who?

BEATRICE: There was hardly a mix-up of rooms.

TITO: There's always a mix-up of rooms on school trips. Especially if you've had a bit to drink.

BEATRICE: And we did have a bit to drink.

TOBIA: I did not mix up the rooms. I am a stickler for that kind of detail. I distinctly remember the arrangement. It was my room, for God's sake.

BEATRICE: Maybe I went to wait in the wrong room.

TOBIA: That's great, that is! Two perfect strangers. (*Pause.*) But that does explain why she – not you, Beatrice, Madame, I mean, but the one I was with – that explains why she insisted I mustn't take off the lion's paw which she seemed to think I was wearing around my neck. She appeared to be excited at the prospect of being scratched on the chest by it. I just thought you were still a bit tight.

BEATRICE: I was, I was just tight somewhere else. But the paw, tell me more about that paw –

TITO: (*Curious.*) Me too.

TOBIA: She was just talking about some fake lion's claw, most likely. You know the kind of juvenile knick-knack.

BEATRICE: (*Anguish increasing. She lifts the section of the parachute which covers her breast and indicates it.*) Touch me here.

TOBIA: Excuse me?

BEATRICE: Please. Here.

TOBIA: I do not believe our revised acquaintance has developed to such a level of intimacy that such a gesture would be appropriate –

BEATRICE: To hell with appropriate! Feel my breasts.

TOBIA: Right. Yes. Good God, may I have look? For purely clinical reasons, you understand. (*Bending down to look. He has trouble focusing.*) Some light, if I may. (*He takes his medical torch.*) Deep, parallel scratches. Four, to be exact. Such as might have been conceivably made by a lion's claw.

BEATRICE: They've never fully healed. I always thought of them as a sign of your passion for me.

TOBIA: Whose, Madame?

BEATRICE: Yours! You! Can we please drop the formality.

TITO: If it's alright with you, I'd like a look too?

TOBIA: This lady is my patient. It would be contrary to medical ethics to let untrained –

TITO: Dad, this lady is my lady, for the time being at least. And I have an idea, and if I could see it –

BEATRICE: Of course you can see it.

TOBIA: It's your choice, but I would like it to be noted that I thoroughly disapprove –

TITO: Just get me the bathroom mirror, Dad.

Pause.

TOBIA: Bon…

Continuing to dither with his 'Bon, bon, bons', TOBIA goes to the bathroom.

TITO: (*To BEATRICE.*) He started saying 'bon' when he had to meet the repayments to the Germans for the retractor. It's a kind of working through of his trauma.

After a few moments TOBIA enters carrying a mirror.

Can I have some light. More to the left –

TOBIA does this.

Hold it just there. Good. Move the light a bit lower, Dad – (*Pause.*) These scars are identical to the ones Aunt Gianna has. And in exactly the same place. No doubt about it. Only she has more of them and they're deeper. Her chest's virtually covered in them.

TOBIA: Aunt Gianna? Flavio's wife? And quite apart from anything else, how the hell would you know?

TITO: I just know, alright.

BEATRICE: Flavio who?

TOBIA: Flavio Ragusa, you must remember him.

BEATRICE: The dunce from 3b?

TOBIA: That's him.

TITO: Yeah, Uncle Flavio.

TOBIA: So correct me if I'm wrong, but the woman whose bed I crawled into and who expected the scratches of this strange talisman, thought she was with Flavio, while he, on the other hand, was not with her but with you, who thought you were with me, who thought I was with you, while all the time I was with the other.

BEATRICE: It's awful!

TOBIA: (*To TITO.*) And then you have to go and tell me about Aunt Gianna?

BEATRICE: So it was Flavio!

TOBIA: So it would seem.

BEATRICE: The bastard. The complete and utter filthy stinking bastard!

TOBIA: You remember him? Back row, next to the window. Tall, fat, semi-albino. My best friend.

TITO: Poor Uncle Flavio –

BEATRICE: Well he is the self same best friend I told you about earlier.

TOBIA: The one who was meant to have told me about the baby?

BEATRICE: The very one.

TOBIA: But that can't be so! I still have the letters which Flavio sent me in Switzerland, letters of undying friendship to comfort me after you'd abandoned me.

TITO: Dad, did you love Mrs Riccobono more than my mother – ?

TOBIA: Mrs Riccobono, indeed! There's another little episode we haven't cleared up –

BEATRICE: What's there to clear up? My novitiate had been terminated. My family only supported me under sufferance, despite the fact that I'd got rid of the baby to keep up appearances. With such a chequered history I felt compelled to take the first hand of friendship held out to me.

TOBIA: I thought you said you carried this Costatino to term – ?

BEATRICE: Got rid of! Not done away with, but got rid of as far as I was concerned. That's where that bastard comes back in. Who knows, perhaps racked by guilt for those nine months of misery I endured carrying the child, he played the part of a faithful friend. He was obviously unable to admit his hand in the affair, but he stood by me all the same.

TOBIA: Stood by you while making me appear the villain of the piece.

BEATRICE: Stood by me, reading from your letters slander which he didn't risk showing me for fear of adding to my misery.

TOBIA: At the same time writing to me – he never minced his words – 'That bitch! She sneers whenever I mention your name!'

BEATRICE: I did mention it, often, but it only made me cry.

TITO: You know, it's kind of embarrassing to hear all this, Dad. Your double life –

TOBIA: What do you mean 'double'? If it was anything, it was simply a former life.

TITO: Well, it's quite a former life. Even Uncle Flavio got in on the action behind Aunt Gianna's back.

TOBIA: Let's leave Aunt Gianna out of this! Quite apart from everything else, she's my sister, and there remains a distinct possibility that I slept with her.

BEATRICE: It is a possibility.

TOBIA: She was already going out with Flavio at the time.

BEATRICE: And you always trusted him?

TOBIA: I never had a reason to distrust him, though it seems I did have but simply didn't know it.

TITO: You even made him my godfather.

TOBIA: It must have been the guilt that drove him to that desperate final act.

BEATRICE: What desperate final act?

TOBIA: You never heard?

TITO: Poor Uncle.

BEATRICE: Dead?

TOBIA: By his own hand.

TITO: Ahh... !

BEATRICE: How horrible!

TITO: I'm sorry, but at this stage it's taken on a life of its own.

BEATRICE: But he wasn't the sort. He always had a solution. When I told him I wanted to terminate, it was he, Flavio, who persuaded me not to, that I'd always regret it. My family wanted me to do it. To terminate. And he stepped in, he stood up for me. For my baby. He had a plan. My family always thought the world of him. And they also knew that he, like you, wanted to study obstetrics –

TOBIA: We did more than study. For ten years we ran a gynaecological practice together.

BEATRICE: Well, perhaps because of these ambitions he asked my family to allow him to see me through the pregnancy, since, according to him, there might be complications. He managed to convince them and I left home under the pretext of having to have some operation whereas, in truth, Flavio took me to his house where, while pretending to be convalescing from the operation, I waited long enough to have the baby.

TOBIA: Costatino!

TITO: Ahhh... !

BEATRICE: Flavio then assured me that Costatino would be brought up in good home, and that was the last I saw of him –

TOBIA: Costatino?

TITO: Ahhh... !

TOBIA: So Flavio took the baby with him? I don't understand.

BEATRICE: He guaranteed me the boy's happiness on condition that I cut forever the umbilical ties. He assured me that it was psychologically for the best that I not return at some later date to upset the boy.

TITO: He probably had him brought up in secret, up north, to be safe, so as not to piss Aunt Gianna off.

TOBIA: (*Slapping him.*) I've told you before about language and leave Aunt Gianna out of this –

BEATRICE: That was the last I saw or heard of Flavio Ragusa. Until today, that is.

TOBIA: Off he went with your son and then nothing more? Quite shocking behaviour!

BEATRICE: All he asked for was a small fee to cover the unavoidable expense of weaning him.

TOBIA: You paid him?

BEATRICE: It was the least I would have done. Even if I had to pull a few fast ones to raise the nine million, eight hundred and sixty thousand lire he needed.

TOBIA: (*Thinking.*) Now I understand why he needed so much money at that time: bringing up a son in secret. He touched me too for some money, for a not unrelated reason. How much did you say he charged you?

BEATRICE: Nine million, eight hundred and sixty thousand.

TOBIA: He asked me for twelve million, eight hundred and forty.

BEATRICE: For what?

TOBIA: To hush up the... the fallout from our affair.

BEATRICE: I hope all that money helped to give my baby a decent upbringing.

TITO: Hang on a second –

TOBIA: What is it now?

TITO: What do you get if you add nine million, eight hundred and sixty to twelve million, eight hundred and forty?

Silence as BEATRICE and TOBIA try to calculate uselessly.

TOBIA: Well, if you know, why don't you tell us?

TITO: Twenty two million, seven hundred thousand lire. Exactly what Uncle Flavio paid, as he often boasted, for 'Grey Arrow', his first bi-plane, which he bought so he could pursue his great passion – which has since become mine – of parachuting.

BEATRICE: The crooked filthy bastard! So that's how he spent my money!

TITO: It all sounds a bit too coincidental to be a coincidence. Ahhh… !

TOBIA: Well, we're into the endgame now. (*To TITO.*) You're sure of this?

TITO: Of course! Don't you remember the story of how he got 'Grey Arrow' for only twenty two million seven hundred. It was a laugh.

TOBIA: I recall the bi-plane, and the figure, vaguely. And it was around the same time. And it was soon after I gave him all my money our practice collapsed.

TITO: It all adds up.

BEATRICE: What kind of monster could exploit a mother's desperation so shamelessly?

TOBIA: And there's something else, Beatrice, I'm afraid there's something else!

BEATRICE: Something else? What else could there be?

TOBIA: Perhaps I shouldn't, but no, it's too late, I've seen the truth.

TITO: Christ! Will we ever get out of this?!

TOBIA: (*Smacking him.*) No blaspheming, you little heathen!

BEATRICE: You tell him!

TITO: (*Plaintively.*) Is simply saying 'Christ' blasphemy?

TOBIA: (*Another two smacks.*) There's two. Next time it will be three.

BEATRICE: Don't keep me dangling like this!

TOBIA: (*To TITO.*) Do you have a drop of whisky?

TITO: (*Peevishly.*) On the bottom shelf.

TOBIA: (*Going to the cabinet.*) I'll never be able to say this unless I have a large one.

TITO: (*Alarmed.*) Dad, speaking of large ones, it's getting bigger.

BEATRICE: Lord Jesus, it's swelling up even more!

TITO: Will someone please tell me why 'Christ' is blasphemous, yet it's fine to say 'Lord Jesus'?

BEATRICE: It's the way you say it.

TITO: His first name's okay, but not his surname?

BEATRICE: It's unjustifiably over-familiar to refer to him simply by his surname. (*To TOBIA.*) Now tell us what you were going to tell us, before I'm torn apart!

TOBIA: (*Having had a drink.*) Right! Bon. I'm ready.

TITO: It's relentless. It just keeps getting bigger.

BEATRICE: Good God, soon I won't be able to turn my head.

TITO: Here we go again. (*A colossal yawn that transforms itself into a liberating cry.*) Aaaaahhhhhh!

BEATRICE: May the Lord have mercy on us!

TOBIA: Amen.

TITO: I need a crowbar, not mercy –

BEATRICE: (*To TOBIA.*) Please say what you have to say –

TOBIA drinks.

TITO: I'm cracking up.

TOBIA: Silence, if you please! I will be brief. (*Brief pause.*) It all boils down to the reason why you gave Flavio Ragusa the aforementioned money. Right. Yes. I said brief, and brief's what I'll be. (*He drinks.*) He knew my heart had been broken; abandoned by the woman I loved, weighed down by the prospect of a future without offspring –

TITO: It's expanding with every contraction! It's bigger than me.

BEATRICE: I can't contain it much longer!!

TOBIA: So he wrote to me. (*He drinks.*) In that sickly sweet prose style of his – sycophantic, I'd call it – I'm sure you know what I mean, Beatrice.

BEATRICE: Hurry up, for the love of God!

TOBIA: 'Do you want a baby?'

BEATRICE: Another?

TOBIA: No, that's what he wrote to me. 'If you want one, you can have one. I got one for you.' Obviously adoption for a bachelor, like myself, was impossible. But I could at least play the part of a father. 'He isn't registered or baptised. You must see him. He's an angel, if you like that sort of thing.'

BEATRICE: (*Quietly.*) O God, the edifice –

TITO: Who? Who was that baby?

TOBIA: You. You were that baby.

BEATRICE: The edifice –

TITO: And this edifice? What's this edifice you keep going on about?

BEATRICE: The edifice of all my illusions, all my beliefs. The edifice has crumbled. The edifice is wrecked.

TITO: Edifice wrecked?! That edifice is me, that edifice is my life. Look what your bungled bed-hopping's done! (*Yawns.*) Ahhh… !

TOBIA: 'Of course I'll need some cash to cover my expenses, after that he's yours, forever.'

TITO: What about the story of my mother's fatal fall while out hunting a month after I was born… ?

TOBIA: I was simply trying to shield you from the truth.

TITO: With the result that I have lived a lie. I don't know who I am any more.

TOBIA: Her son, that's who you are.

BEATRICE: Is it not enough that we must know the truth without having to say it?

TITO: And therefore you are not my father?

TOBIA: You could look at it this way; you might have lost a father, but you've gained a mother.

TITO: And I am my own brother!

BEATRICE: Costatino!

TITO: Who's he?

BEATRICE: You!

TOBIA: It's been staring us in the face all along. Costatino was her favourite emperor, Tito was mine.

TITO: And I but a compromise of your ancient history.

TOBIA: But our ancient history isn't what it used to be. Therefore, there is nothing left for me now but to retire gracefully.

TITO: Ahhh... ! Not even the efforts of the combined armed forces could dig me out. I'm frightened. I'm really frightened.

BEATRICE: I don't feel anything any more.

TOBIA: What about me? Not only have I been forced to confront my physical inadequacies, but also my professional failings. I'll call an ambulance. There's nothing else for it.

TOBIA goes to the phone. Pause.

TITO: Hey... Mum, how do you think my stepfather, Mr Riccobono, will take it? (*Silence.*) Is he the understanding type? I'll come and live with you and we'll never be separated again. Ahhh... !

BEATRICE: (*Murmuring to herself in prayer.*) Blessed Eustace who was so mild and yet put his body through every torture, was martyred and suffered death. So if it pleased God to grant him eternal rest, may he look mercifully on the prayers of the sinner and grant her absolution in this – what did you say? Mum? Did you call me Mum?

TOBIA: (*Returning.*) They're on their way.

Silence. TITO messes with a section of the parachute, while BEATRICE continues with her prayer.

TITO: And that also means that my godfather is my father.

TOBIA: Will you stop it?!

TITO: Now I understand why me and Uncle Flavio got on so well. He was my dad. My real dad.

TOBIA: (*Giving him a smack.*) Just stop it right now, Mister!

TITO: All the smacks in the world can't change the truth... Uncle.

TOBIA: (*Smacking him again.*) But it was me, me, me who cooked for you, cleaned for you, looked after you. It was me who paid for your education –

TITO: Just stocking-fillers, compared to the gift of life. And you did not give me that.

TOBIA: (*Raining TITO with blows which he stoically accepts.*) Enough! Enough! Enough!

TOBIA starts sobbing.

BEATRICE: And you, Blessed Virgin, who have never failed to care for the abject and tormented –

TITO continues to manically fold and furl a section of the parachute on his mother's back.

TITO: (*Folding.*) Exterior right hand strip over interior left hand –

TOBIA: What on earth are you doing now?

TITO: – then lay the strips like an accordion. Still brings tears to my eyes. That last time, when my father, Uncle Flavio, took me with him. That awful time.

TOBIA: What about that time?

TITO: It was our first parachute jump together. It should have been the first of many. I was so excited. I said to him: 'Uncle, guess who folded and packed your parachute today? I did.' 'You?' he said. 'But you hate doing it nearly as much as I do. You won't even do your own.' You see, packing a parachute is boring as hell. Real parachutists hate it, but that day I was so happy that I did it for him.

BEATRICE: – the sorrow Blessed Eustace felt after he'd sound the trumpet –

TOBIA: You folded it? You packed it?

TITO: Yes, it was me, me who won't even make my own bed. I understand it now, because he was my father –

TOBIA: So he didn't consciously kill himself on that jump? Don't you know what you've just said? You killed him! You murdered Flavio!

TITO: Ahh… !That's a lie! He was my father. How could you say that?

TOBIA: I can say it because your uncle went plummeting to the ground not by his own decision, but by your utter ineptitude. Don't you remember, at the inquest, it was discovered that the parachute was packed in such a way that it could never open? And this is why it was believed that he wanted to do it, to top himself, but no… !

TITO: But I spent half the night packing that parachute.

TOBIA: Go to the police records and see for yourself. (*Indicating the section of parachute folded by*